SOCCER
The Right Technique

For
Parents*Coaches*Teachers*Youth Leaders
How to Coach Age 10 and Under

by
T.J. Martin
Professional British Soccer Coach

© 1996 Thomas J. Martin

TRT SPORTS & PUBLISHING

All rights reserved. Published 1996

Printed in the United States of America

ISBN 0-9651691-0-3

All photography, including front and back cover,
by Paul K. Buck, Dallas, Texas
Front cover, design and production by Armstrong Creative, Dallas, Texas
All illustrations by Greg Contestabile, Dallas, Texas
Edited by Carla R. Springer, Dallas, Texas
Printed by McKool Graphics, Dallas, Texas

TABLE OF CONTENTS

TABLE OF CONTENTS

TABLE OF CONTENTS

ACKNOWLEDGMENT

In writing this book I am greatly indebted to several people who have been very supportive and encouraging. My mom and dad, my Aunt Rosie, Aunt Norah, and all my aunts and uncles (of which there are many!). Ian Green, for helping me get my start in Dallas; Joanna Green and Tina Flohr, for helping me put this book together. Paul K. Buck, for his unending patience and excellent photography work. Greg Contestabile, for his perfection on the illustrations. Jerry Maley, a good friend and great coach with whom I've had the pleasure of working here in the USA. Also, my good friend Don Shanks, a great soccer player on one of the most exciting teams of the 70's: Queens Park Rangers, London, England. But most importantly of all I would like to thank my lovely wife and very best friend, Ann Martin.

In addition to the people stated above I'd also like to sincerely thank Betty Guilliams, Athletic Director of the June Shelton School and Evaluation Center, Dallas, Texas. The Shelton School is primarily dedicated to teaching children with learning differences. Having the opportunity to coach soccer at a school of this caliber was truly one of the greatest experiences of my coaching career and one that will not soon be forgotten.

INTRODUCTION

This book is about demonstrating and teaching the very basic skills and The Right Technique of soccer to children 10 years of age and under.

It has been formatted in a style in which the children in Europe learn how to perform and call correctly by name each specific move and technique related to running with the ball, turning, passing, receiving and ball control, dribbling, shooting, and heading.

As this book has been specifically designed to demonstrate and teach The Right Technique of soccer, what you will NOT find in this book is a great deal of instructional reading. What you will find are instructional photographs and sketches which will show in sequential order, with easy to understand instructions for each sketch or sequence of photographs. This enables children of this particular age group to more easily duplicate the material shown, and hopefully, make their learning more fun. By teaching The Right Technique and correct terminology to children of this age group I have found they respond more favorably to the game as they have been taught correctly early on. I strongly recommend that each player have his or her own book, and to mark his or her own scores (given by the coach) at the end of each practice session.

The basic skills shown in this book can be taught to children from all walks of life, including those with learning disabilities or minor handicaps. It has been my experience as a professional soccer coach that these children react quite well to the game of soccer as it has greatly improved their listening skills, duplication skills, balance, and most important of all, their self-esteem.

Good luck to you all!

To Coaches, Teachers, Youth Leaders, and Parents

Soccer is easily the most popular sport in the world. It is played in more countries than you can imagine. In fact, just about every nation in the world plays soccer. The sport has its own worldwide organization called FIFA. This abbreviation stands for Federation International of Football Association ("football" is another name for soccer). There are almost as many countries in FIFA as there are in the United Nations. In international soccer, the laws of the game are the same all over the world. Even though the rules do not change from one nation to another, the way each nation actually plays the game can be very different. This is because each nation has developed its own style of play over the years. For example, the English style relies on quick short passes and hard tackling. Brazilians, on the other hand, are known for their tremendous ball control skills. Their warm climate has developed a slower paced game where players save their bursts of speed for when they really need it. The United States, meanwhile, has long been considered the "sleeping giant" of the soccer world, but the giant is stirring. In the decade of the 80's, youth soccer participation has doubled in the United States. Today, 15 million kids, all under the age of 18, are playing what the whole world calls the "beautiful game."

Over the past four years, top United States players are being sought by professional teams around the world. You can be part of the success of the United States or any other country just by refereeing or coaching. Who knows, one of your players could be one of the stars who will represent his or her country in the future.

This book is all about development, The Right Technique, and basic skills for the young players. It is about making learning fun and contains mostly photos of players demonstrating the correct technique of the basic skills used in the game. To myself and millions, soccer is the greatest game in the world and the most exciting. When young players learn The Right Technique and basic skills early, they will get better in every game, and you will see the pleasure they get when they execute the many moves using skillful technique in their play. With this book you will discover which technique they can perform better than others and which will need to be improved upon, but most important of all is that you practice as much as you can and also have fun.

Remember, you do not have to be a professional soccer player to teach The Right Technique. Just study this book and follow the photographs step-by-step, then demonstrate The Right Technique to the kids. Eventually, with each practice, their technique will improve.

SOCCER *is not coming to* AMERICA

It is already here!

TO ALL YOUNG PLAYERS

I have developed this book as a soccer education for you. This book is about developing your ability in the critical soccer techniques of

* RUNNING WITH THE BALL
* PASSING
* TURNING
* RECEIVING AND BALL CONTROL
* DRIBBLING
* SHOOTING
* HEADING
* THROWING THE BALL INTO PLAY

To focus your attention toward these techniques and for you to be able to measure your progress, I have developed a series of enjoyable challenges for you. To master the techniques and to score highly on the soccer test follow this program:

* Watch as many soccer games on television as you can. Study the moves and techniques that the players perform.
* Study the photographs and instructions in this book and practice as much as possible.
* To assess your ability test yourself or ask to be tested by your coach, teacher, parent, or youth leader.
* You will now discover which techniques you can perform better than others and which need to be improved.
* Have fun by following the recommended practices in this book.
* While parents, teachers, and coaches can help you, you must take responsibility for your progress by practicing as much as possible.

Strive to improve your performance and those techniques you need to develop.

SOCCER CODE OF CONDUCT

1. Learn the laws of the game.
2. Do not argue with the referee or linesman.
3. Always be punctual, polite, and have a good appearance.
4. Be a modest winner and be able to take defeat graciously.
5. Always keep your self control.

If you follow the code you will be a credit to your club, school, parents, and yourself.

REMEMBER
Soccer Builds
CHARACTER!

RUNNING WITH THE BALL

When first playing soccer most young players just run, chase, and kick the soccer ball. However, it is very important to learn how to run quickly with the ball while keeping it under control. It is a very important and valuable technique.

RUNNING WITH THE BALL

Technique

1. When running with the ball, play the ball well out in front of you. This technique allows you to run much faster while at the same time enables you to lift your head.

2. When running with the ball, play with your instep (laces).

3. To cover ground more quickly, take a few long touches. The more times you touch the ball, the slower you will run.

RUNNING WITH THE BALL

DRILL FOR RUNNING WITH THE BALL

1. Two teams race against each other to cones or flags placed 30 yards out, by running with the ball using The Right Technique.

2. The coach watches each player to see if they are using The Right Technique, i.e. using the laces, playing the ball well in front, and keeping the head up.

Technique

1. Play the ball with the laces.

2. Play the ball well in front, while keeping it as straight as possible.

3. Keep looking up.

PASSING

The most important technique in soccer is passing. Young players must learn the basic technique of passing very early.

PASSING

PUSH PASS:

The most reliable technique for passing the ball on the ground with accuracy over short distances.

Technique

1. The kicking foot is turned outward so that the inside of the foot makes contact with the middle of the ball.

2. Eyes should be looking down at the ball and the head should be steady.

3. Follow through with the kicking foot.

4. Arms spread for balance.

5. DO NOT TOE THE BALL!

LOW DRIVEN PASS:
The technique for passing the ball over long distances

Technique

1. Look down at the ball.

2. Play the ball with laces.

3. Follow through with the kicking foot.

4. DO NOT TOE THE BALL!

PASSING

DRILLS FOR PASSING

PUSH PASS - DRILL A

A. Each player with a partner 10 yards apart. Passing the ball back and forth to each other, using the push pass.

B. The coach watches for The Right Technique, i.e. kicking with the inside of the foot, eyes on the ball and arms up for balance. Make sure players control the ball before passing back, i.e. foot trap or the inside of the foot control.

Technique

1. Head should be still.

2. Eyes on the ball.

3. Follow through with the kicking foot.

4. Arms spread for balance.

5. Kick through the middle of the ball with the inside of the foot.

DRILLS FOR PASSING

PUSH PASS - DRILL B

A. Three players in a square, 12 x 12 yards. One player in the middle must try to intercept the pass. See how many times you can pass the ball to each other without the player in the middle getting the ball.

B. The coach watches for The Right Technique and also the movement of the player receiving the pass.

Technique

1. Head should be still.

2. Eyes on the ball.

3. Follow through with the kicking foot.

4. Arms spread for balance.

5. Kick through the middle of the ball with the inside of the foot.

PASSING

DRILLS FOR PASSING

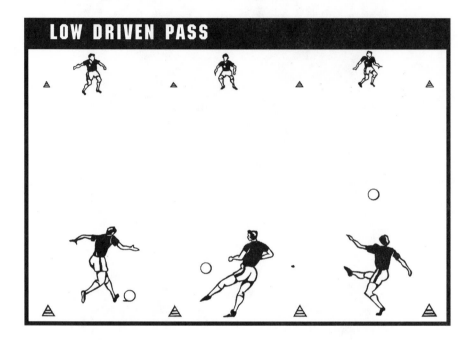

LOW DRIVEN PASS

A. Players practice long passes 30 yards apart.

B. Try to keep the ball low.

C. The coach watches for The Right Technique, i.e. play the ball with the laces and follow through with the kicking foot.

Technique

1. Look down at the ball.

2. Play the ball with the laces.

3. Follow through with the kicking foot.

4. DO NOT TOE THE BALL!

TURNING: CHANGING DIRECTION

Changing direction is the next skill young players need to know. Therefore, they must learn The Right Technique and basic turns that are used at the highest level. There are six turns that are used in professional soccer all over the world. Each turn will take many hours of practice to master, but once learned will greatly improve his/her game. For ages 8 and under the recommended turns to be taught are the Stop Turn and the Drag Back. Ages 9 and up should be taught to master all six turns. Players, master each turn and you will see your game improve tremendously.

Each turn has a name;
try to remember each one!

TURNING

THE STOP TURN

Technique

1. Move the ball slowly in one direction.
2. Stop the ball with the sole of the right foot.

THE STOP TURN

Technique

3. Turn quickly; play the ball with the same foot in the opposite direction.

4. Bend your knees.

5. Accelerate away after the turn.

TURNING

THE DRAG BACK

Technique

1. Move the ball slowly in one direction.
2. Turn the ball under the body by dragging the ball in the opposite direction with the sole of your right foot.

THE DRAG BACK

Technique

3. Turn quickly; play the ball with the same foot in the opposite direction.

4. Bend your knees.

5. Accelerate away.

TURNING

THE INSIDE HOOK

Technique

1. Move the ball slowly in one direction.
2. Reach and hook the ball with the inside of your right foot and move in the opposite direction.

THE INSIDE HOOK

Technique

3. Bend your knees.
4. Accelerate away.

TURNING

THE OUTSIDE HOOK

Technique

1. Move the ball slowly in one direction.

2. Reach and hook the ball with the outside of your right foot and move in the opposite direction.

TURNING

THE OUTSIDE HOOK

Technique

3. Bend your knees.

4. Accelerate away.

TURNING

THE STEP OVER

Technique

1. Move the ball slowly in one direction.

2. Step over the ball low and quickly with your right foot.

3. Swivel your hips and play the ball back in the opposite direction with the inside of your other foot.

THE STEP OVER

Technique

4. Bend your knees

5. Accelerate away.

TURNING

THE CRUYFF

This turn has been created by the famous Dutch soccer player,
Johan Cruyff.

Technique

1. Move the ball slowly in one direction.

2. Turn your right foot inward with your toe down and push the ball
behind and away from you in the opposite direction.

TURNING

THE CRUYFF

Technique

3. Bend your knees.

4. Accelerate away.

TURNING

DRILLS FOR TURNING

1. Each player is in a square 10 x 10 yards with a ball.

2. Practice each turn.

3. The coach watches to see if the players are using The Right Technique, i.e. moving the ball slowly, turning quickly, bending the knees, and accelerating away.

DRILLS FOR TURNING

1. Players move the ball slowly toward the cones or flags 20 yards apart.

2. Coach blows the whistle before the player reaches the cones or flags.

3. Players then use one of the six turns and accelerates back, or the coach decides which turn to use.

RECEIVING & BALL CONTROL

Players receive the ball in a game at various speeds, heights, angles, and directions. You must learn The Right Technique to control these balls then prepare them quickly for their next touch. Concentrate and keep your eyes on the ball in order to be able to pass the ball quickly.

RECEIVING & BALL CONTROL

INSIDE OF THE FOOT CONTROL

When the ball is coming toward you fast and hard the best way to stop the pace of the ball and get it under control for passing quickly is by using the inside of your foot.

Technique

1. Use the inside of the foot to stop the ball.

2. Keep your eyes on the ball.

3. Keep your arms spread for balance.

RECEIVING & BALL CONTROL

FOOT TRAP

Technique

1. Use the sole of the foot.

2. Wedge the ball between the ground and the sole of your foot.

3. Keep your arms spread for balance.

RECEIVING & BALL CONTROL

THIGH CONTROL

Technique

1. Throw the ball in the air to chin height.
2. Get your thigh in line with the ball.
3. Cushion the ball with your thigh.
4. Catch the ball, repeat steps 1 through 3 several times for practice.
5. Keep your head still.
6. Keep your eyes on the ball.
7. Keep your arms up for balance.

DO NOT USE YOUR KNEE!

RECEIVING & BALL CONTROL

DRILLS FOR RECEIVING & CONTROL

Practice for the Foot Trap and Thigh Control

Each player holds the ball out in front of him/her. The player drops the ball and practices trapping the ball with the foot trap and the thigh control technique.

Technique

1. Head should be still.

2. Eyes on the ball.

3. Arms spread for balance.

RECEIVING & BALL CONTROL

DRILLS FOR FOOT & THIGH CONTROL

Players get in pairs facing each other 10 yards apart. One player throws the ball at various heights. The partner then controls the ball with the thigh or a foot trap and passes it back to the thrower.

Technique

1. Keep your arms up for balance.

2. Keep your eyes on the ball.

DRIBBLING

Dribbling is one of the most exciting techniques in soccer. It is all about the quickness of the feet and good balance. You must learn where and when to dribble, when to fake (make the defender lose balance), and adopt a positive approach to dribbling. Do not dribble in or around your own penalty box as this will make it easier for the opposing team to score if you lose possession of the ball. Be confident!

SOCCER'S WHITE KNIGHT

Perhaps more than any soccer star who ever played, Sir Stanley Matthews of England proved that you do not have to score many goals to contribute royally to winning games. The Wizard of the Dribble, as he is still known at the age of 79, has given a rich legacy that has spanned decades and continents. Off the field he contributed greatly to soccer's global popularity as a coach and ambassador of the sport. Citing brilliant ball playing skills on the field and his efforts to promote the game internationally, Queen Elizabeth II knighted the game's right winger in 1965. Sir Stanley hopes young players will rediscover the importances of ball control. "My style of dribbling still works, and the player that can dribble is going to cause many problems for the defense," said Sir Stanley.

One of the proudest moments in my life was being asked to play in a celebrity game for Sir Stanley Matthews, pictured above on the left.

MATTHEW'S MOVE

Even though these three moves are illustrated for right footed players, each move should also be practiced and adapted using the left foot.

Technique

1. Move the ball with the inside of your right foot to your left side and then fake to go to your left by leaning to the left.

2. Bend your knees and move your right foot quickly behind the ball

3. Accelerate away with your right foot to push the ball forward and past the marker.

Technique

1. Play the ball out in front of you.

2. Swing your right foot around the ball leaning to the right.

3. Bend your knees. Push the ball past the marker using your left foot and accelerate away.

DOUBLE TOUCH

Technique

1. Play the ball to your right with your left foot.

2. Push the ball with the inside of your right foot

3. Accelerate past the marker.

DRILLS FOR DRIBBLING

DRILL A

Players should be 10 yards apart. Players move toward the cone practicing one of the dribbling moves, i.e. Matthews, Scissors, or Double Touch, going past the cone and coming back to the line.

Technique

1. Fake and disguise.

2. Bend your knees.

3. Aim for the space behind the defender.

4. Accelerate away.

DRIBBLING

DRILLS FOR DRIBBLING

DRILL B

Player "A" moves toward player "B" using one of the dribbling moves, i.e. Matthews, Scissors or Double Touch, to get to the other side.

Technique

1. Fake and disguise.

2. Bend your knees.

3. Aim for the space behind the defender.

4. Accelerate away.

SHOOTING

In Shooting, emphasis should be placed on timing, accuracy, and power. Young players should learn which part of the foot to shoot with and how to shoot with either foot. They must learn how to turn and shoot under pressure. Also, they should not be afraid to shoot when they have a chance. A bit of advice to young players: you may not score every time you shoot, but you will not score if you do not shoot.

SHOOTING

Technique

1. Place your non-kicking foot beside the ball keeping your head still and over the ball.

2. Keep your ankle extended and hit through the middle of the ball with the laces.

3. Keep your head down. The head comes up automatically as you follow through.

4. Follow through with your kicking foot.

5. DO NOT TOE THE BALL!

SHOOTING TOWARD
THE GOAL

Technique

1. Always aim for the far post when shooting from a wide angle.

2. Strike through the middle of the ball using the laces.

3. Keep your head down.

4. DO NOT TOE THE BALL!

SHOOTING

DRILLS FOR SHOOTING

DRILL A

1. The coach passes the ball to the player on the left and then to the player on the right.

2. Coach watches for The Right Technique, i.e. shooting with the laces, head still, and follow through.

3. Practice shooting with the left and right foot.

SHOOTING

DRILLS FOR SHOOTING

DRILL B

1. Players line the ball up on the edge of the box.

2. Each player takes a shot at the goal, one at a time. Each player will try to beat the goal keeper.

3. For younger children, put the balls closer.

HEADING

Heading is an important skill because a large part of the game is played at or above head height. Children must learn The Right Technique of attacking the ball with the forehead. DO NOT let the ball bounce off your head; attack it with force. Players must be able to head for clearance, head to pass, and head to score.

Technique

1. Use your forehead.

2. Head through the middle of the ball.

3. Keep your eyes open.

4. Attack the ball, feet apart, and use your arms for balance and power.

HEADING

DRILLS FOR HEADING

1. Coach puts players in pairs five yards apart. One player throws the ball under arm up for the other player who tries to head the ball back into the thrower's arms.

2. Each player throws ten balls.

3. Coach watches for The Right Technique, i.e. one leg in front of the other slightly apart, attacking the ball, heading with your forehead, arms up for balance.

HEADING

DRILLS FOR HEADING

DRILL B

1. Two teams 2 vs 2 heading competition. Partners are 10 yards apart; each team tries to score a goal by heading.

2. One player from each team throws the ball up for his/her partner who tries to score past the other team. Players are allowed to catch the ball.

3. Players must stay on their own goal line.

4. Coach watches for The Right Technique, i.e. one leg in front of the other, slightly apart, attacking the ball, heading with your forehead, arms up for balance.

5. The first team to score five goals is the winner.

HEADING

DRILLS FOR HEADING

DRILL C - THE HEAD CATCH GAME

1. Players line up in front of the coach. Coach throws the ball to the first player under arm, then calls "head" or "catch." The player has to do the opposite of what is called, i.e. "head", then he/she catches the ball, "catch", then he/she would head the ball.

2. If the player does the wrong response, the player sits down, Coach then keeps going on down the line.

3. All the players who are still in the game take one step forward. The coach steps backward and starts again, until there is one remaining player who is the winner.

4. Coach watches for The Right Technique, i.e. heading with your forehead, arms up for balance, and attacking the ball.

This game is great fun and is important in developing listening skills.

THROWING IN THE BALL

If an opponent kicks the ball over the touch line, your team will be awarded a Throw In. This is taken at the point where the ball crossed the line. You must throw the ball with both hands from behind your head, and both feet must be touching the ground on or behind the touch line. To ensure your team keeps possession of the ball try to throw to an unguarded player. If all players are guarded try to throw it to the player who has the best chance of passing it back to you.

THROWING IN THE BALL

THE RIGHT TECHNIQUE FOR THROWING THE BALL INTO PLAY

1. Touch the back of your neck with the ball.

2. Clasp the ball tightly.

3. Throw the ball smoothly over your head.

THROWING IN THE BALL

THE RIGHT TECHNIQUE FOR THROWING THE BALL INTO PLAY

Technique

1. Make sure your hands are clasped tightly on the ball.

2. Touch the back of your neck with the ball and throw the ball smoothly over your head toward your player.

3. Make sure you keep both feet on the ground. Do not lift your feet up as you throw or it will be a foul throw and the ball will be given to your opponent.

4. Make sure your feet do not cross over the touch line.

COMPONENTS OF A PRACTICE SESSION

Practices are the ideal place to correct mistakes, become physically trained for competition, practice game technique and tactics, and get ready for the next contest.

Each practice session should include the following:

1. Warm-up stretches

2. Introduce and practice a new skill

3. Review and practice previously taught skills

4. Fitness training, i.e. races, etc.

5. Practice in game situations

6. Ending with 15 or 20 minutes of game playing with 3 vs. 3, 4 vs. 4, 5 vs. 5, etc.

1. WARM-UP

Warm-ups should be the first part of each practice. It is very important for younger players to realize that they must loosen their muscles, no matter what age. Warming up means to gradually prepare the body for vigorous intense activity. For example, have players dribble the ball, jog, and stretch for at least 10 to 15 minutes prior to practice.

2. HAVE A PLAN

The most important practice consideration is to plan sessions so that you create the environment you want and to accomplish the goals you set. This means you must know what you want to accomplish then design your practice to get it done. Be sure to determine the time you need for each phase of practice.

3. MAKE PRACTICES FUN

Fun means keeping the practice session moving and enjoyable. Hard work can be fun. The key is to find what exercises the players enjoy. When you find them do not overdo them to a point of reducing the thrill. Rather move on to other exercises so players will look forward to the other drills.

4. CONTINUALLY REVIEW SKILLS AND TECHNIQUE

Children may remember general instructions but need reminders of specifics as you introduce new skills and techniques. You will also need to review them. The job of the instructor is to identify technically weak areas and educate players. Encourage your players to help coach each other. Review techniques and show players how to improve, but make them responsible for their own skill development.

5. TEST SHEETS

Use the test sheets at the end of each practice. Always give players their scores for that lesson. Remember, children of this age can be quite sensitive to peer pressure, therefore, it is recommended that the coach use discretion when giving the children their scores.

6. POINTERS FOR COACHES

WINNING: Please do not demand a child to WIN.

LOSING: Do not blame or criticize if he or she LOSES.

If you lose, **YOU BOUNCE BACK.**

NURSERY COURSE PRACTICE SESSION 5-7 YEARS OLD

It is very important to remember that the techniques and games in this book are not set in stone. They are here to give guidelines as to the kinds of direction children of this age gain most benefit.

When working on a Nursery Course there are many "extras" to take into consideration. For example, do not take for granted that the children have played soccer or even kicked a soccer ball. Or that they know their left foot from their right, the inside of the foot from the outside of the foot, or even know how to count.

With this in mind it is important to make each demonstration as basic as possible. Give the children only one thing at a time to think about. Keep EVERYTHING simple, even to the extent of explaining how goals are scored. Believe it or not, some kids do not know.

The aim of this book is to teach The Right Technique early and have lots of fun learning.

PRACTICE DRILLS AND FUN GAMES

SOCCER GAME

SMALL SIDED WORLD CUP
3 vs 3   4 vs 4   5 vs 5

It is very important to remember that when you finish each practice always end with 20 to 25 minutes of a small sided game, i.e. 3 vs 3, 4 vs 4, 5 vs 5.

The reason for this is that players get lots of contact with the ball and should be encouraged to try the new techniques they have learned, i.e. turns, dribbling moves, and passing. Also, players should spread out to receive the ball for passing and moving.

Coaches should make it as fun as possible, i.e. giving team names like USA vs Brazil, England vs Scotland, etc. This generates a lot of excitement.

HITTING THE CONES

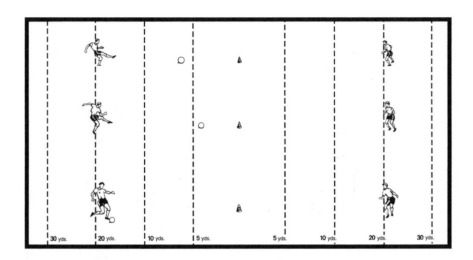

30 yds. 20 yds. 10 yds. 5 yds. 5 yds. 10 yds. 20 yds. 30 yds.

A. MINUTES: 15 to 20

B. ORGANIZATION: Players get in pairs with one ball and attempt to knock down the cone. Starting from 5 yards, going to 10 yards, 20 then 30. The Coach gives the command to "Go" and players try to knock down the cone. The first pair to knock the cone down five times wins.

C. COACH: Watches for The Right Technique, i.e. using the inside of the foot (Push Pass) from 5, 10, and 20 yards and using the laces from 30 yards.

SOCCER GOLF

A. MINUTES: 30 (Groups of 4)

B. ORGANIZATION: Place 8 to 10 cones or flags (for holes) different lengths apart. Each player uses a ball. Just like in golf they must hit the cones with the least amount and best pass possible.

C. COACH: Watches for The Right Technique, i.e. Push Pass for short distance, Low Driven Pass for long distance.

MONKEY IN THE MIDDLE

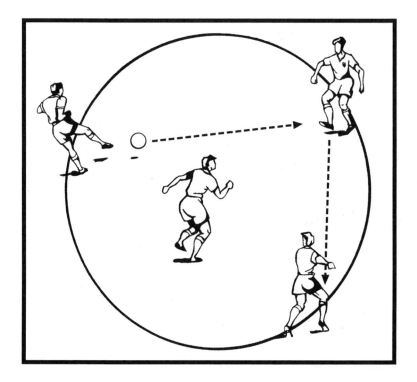

A. MINUTES: 10 to 15

B. ORGANIZATION: Players get in a circle about 30 feet diameter. One
player goes in the middle. Players on the outside pass to each other.
The player in the middle must try to intercept the pass. The player
whose pass is intercepted then goes in the middle.

C. COACH: Watches for The Right Technique, i.e. ball control, passing
with the inside of the foot, and disguising the pass.

TURNING RACES

A. MINUTES: 10 to 15

B. ORGANIZATION: Players race toward the cones 30 yards away, executing one of the six turns in between the cones. The players then race back to the starting point.

C. COACH: Watches for The Right Technique, i.e. turning quickly, bending the knees, running with the ball, and using the laces.

CRABS & DRIBBLERS

A. MINUTES: 10 to 15

B. ORGANIZATION: Players with the ball dribble past the crabs and try to get to the other side. The crabs try to kick the ball out of the square. The dribbler left with the ball at the end is the winner.

C. COACH: Watches for The Right Technique in dribbling, i.e. Matthew's Move, Double Touch, and Scissors. This is also good for turn technique.

KING OF THE SQUARE

A. MINUTES: 10 to 15

B. ORGANIZATION: Each player has a ball. The players will start dribbling inside of the square. When the coach says "Go", players then try to kick out each other's ball. The last player who keeps the ball in the square is the winner.

C. COACH: Watches for The Right Technique, i.e. turning with the ball, dribbling, and ball control.

FOLLOW THE LEADER

A. MINUTES: 10

B. ORGANIZATION: Players are in pairs. The lead player dribbles and runs with the ball anywhere on the field. His/her partner trys to copy and shadows him.

C. COACH: Watches for The Right Technique in dribbling, i.e. Matthews' Move, Double Touch, and Scissors.

PASSING THROUGH THE LEGS

A. MINUTES: 12

B. ORGANIZATION: Partners stand approximately 5 yards apart. One will stand with legs apart. The partner then attempts to pass the ball through with the inside of the foot (Push Pass). The partner passing will then move on to another player and do the same.

C. COACH: Watches for The Right Technique, i.e. using the inside of the foot (Push pass), keep the head still and arms spread.

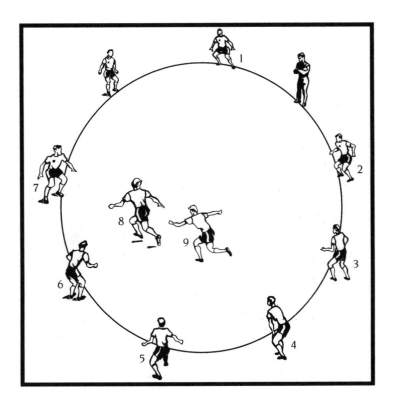

A. MINUTES: 15 to 20 (No ball used in this drill).

B. ORGANIZATION: Players form a circle. Each player has a number. When the coach calls two numbers the first number is the mouse and the second is the cat. The cat has to tag the mouse. The mouse cannot go outside the circle. There can also be two mice in the middle at the same time.

C. COACH: Watches the players for turning, twisting, burst of speed, and fakes.

BEAT THE KEEPER

A. MINUTES: 10 to 15

B. ORGANIZATION: Two players and one goalkeeper. One player throws the ball. The other player tries to head past the keeper. Ten throws each, then they rotate.

C. COACH: Watches for The Right Technique, i.e. attacking the ball using their forehead, arms up for balance, and legs slightly apart.

JACK IN THE BOX

JUMPING HEADERS

A. MINUTES: 10 to 15

B. ORGANIZATION: Players get in threes 10 yards apart. Two players have soccer balls; one person in the middle. The throwers throw the soccer ball one at a time toward the middle player who heads the ball back. The middle player then turns quickly to face the other thrower. One minute in the middle then the players rotate.

C. COACH: Watches for the throwers throwing the ball in properly and the headers using The Right Technique, i.e. attacking the ball and arms up for balance.

SOCCER TENNIS

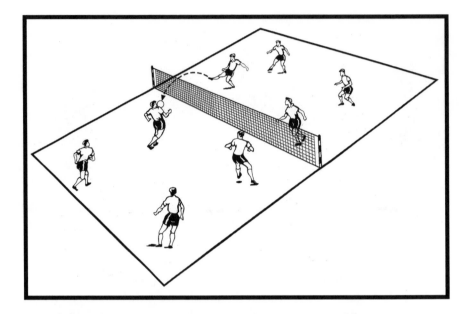

A. MINUTES: 15 to 20 (Recommended for 10 years or older)

B. ORGANIZATION: Court size of 20 x 40 yards, divided in half. Two teams of four stand on opposite sides of a waist high net. One team starts the game by serving (kicking) from the back line over the net. The opposing team must try to get the ball back over the net by heading or kicking it. They are allowed only one bounce. If the ball does bounce twice before going back over the net or goes out of bounds, the ball is dead and the serving team gets the point.

C. COACH: Watches for The Right Technique, i.e. heading, chest, and thigh control. Good ball control.

PASS & CONTROL

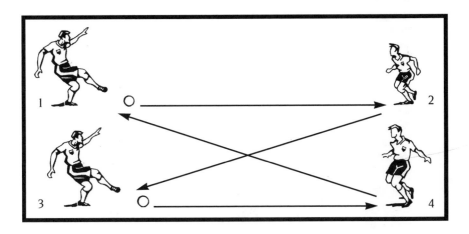

A. MINUTES: 10 to 15

B. ORGANIZATION: Four players, 15 yards apart. Player 1 passes to Player 2 who controls the ball using The Right Technique; i.e. the inside of the foot for fast hard balls, or the foot trap for slow easy balls. Then Player 2 passes to Player 3, then 3 to 4, who then passes back to Player 1. Repeat this drill for 10 to 15 minutes.

C. COACH: Watches for The Right Technique, i.e. push pass, receiving and ball control.

THE RIGHT TECHNIQUE CHART

The Coach gives scores out of 4.

4 pt *Excellent*

3 pt *Very Good*

2 pt *Good*

1 pt *Needs Improvement*

Players must try to beat their scores each practice.

NAME	WEEK 1 RUNNING WITH THE BALL	WEEK 2 PASSING	WEEK 3 TURNING	WEEK 4 RECEIVING & BALL CONTROL	WEEK 5 DRIBBLING	WEEK 6 SHOOTING	WEEK 7 HEADING	WEEK 8 THROW IN	TOTAL SCORE

ABOUT THE AUTHOR

Thomas (Tommy) J. Martin is a native of Newcastle, England, who has been coaching soccer professionally in the United States for 12 years. He holds an "A" coaching license from the United Kingdom and now specializes in coaching children age 10 and under. Being a top skills coach, he has successfully and consistently developed players from recreation league standard to classic league standard, many of whom went on to win soccer scholarships. Tommy has also been involved with coaching in the Olympics Development Program in Dallas, Texas. He has coached in Los Angeles and Santa Monica, California, as well as Dallas, Texas. Tommy has had tremendous success coaching children with learning differences.

Dear Soccer Enthusiast,

I hope that you have read and enjoyed "Soccer, The Right Technique," and can apply it to your game. I recommend that each team player as well as the coach have his/her own copy of this book.

If you are a coach, I hope that you will encourage your players to study "Soccer, The Right Technique" and to practice as much as possible. If you are a parent, I encourage you to study and practice with your children in order for them to become the best players they can be.

Remember, soccer is a fun and challenging game for all age groups and a sport in which the entire family can participate.

All the best,

J. J. Marto

ORDER FORM

To order "Soccer, The Right Technique" send your check or money order for $14.95 plus $2.50 per book shipping and handling, or $1.25 per book shipping and handling for orders of 12 books or more, to:

"Soccer, The Right Technique"
1164 Bishop St., Suite 124 Box 1
Honolulu, Hawaii 96813

PLEASE PRINT:

Name_____

Address_____Apt. #_____

City_____State_____Zip_____

Telephone Number (   )_____

QTY	TITLE	UNIT PRICE	TOTAL
	Soccer, The Right Technique	$14.95	
	Postage & Handling ($2.50 per book, $1.25 per book for orders of 12 or more)		
	Hawaii residents add 4% sales tax		
	Please allow 4 to 6 weeks for delivery.	TOTAL	

WATCH FOR T. J. MARTIN'S UPCOMING BOOK TITLED, "GOALKEEPING UNDER TEN, THE RIGHT TECHNIQUE," WHICH IS SCHEDULED FOR RELEASE IN NOVEMBER, 1996.

_____CHECK HERE AND RETURN IF YOU WOULD LIKE INFORMATION ON "SOCCER, THE RIGHT TECHNIQUE" VIDEO OR THE BOOK "GOALKEEPING UNDER TEN, THE RIGHT TECHNIQUE."

ORDER FORM

To order "Soccer, The Right Technique" send your check or money order for $14.95 plus $2.50 per book shipping and handling, or $1.25 per book shipping and handling for orders of 12 books or more, to:

"Soccer, The Right Technique"
1164 Bishop St., Suite 124 Box 1
Honolulu, Hawaii 96813

PLEASE PRINT:

Name_____

Address_____Apt. #_____

City_____State_____Zip_____

Telephone Number (   )_____

QTY	TITLE	UNIT PRICE	TOTAL
	Soccer, The Right Technique	$14.95	
	Postage & Handling ($2.50 per book, $1.25 per book for orders of 12 or more)		
	Hawaii residents add 4% sales tax		
	Please allow 4 to 6 weeks for delivery. TOTAL		

WATCH FOR T. J. MARTIN'S UPCOMING BOOK TITLED, "GOALKEEPING UNDER TEN, THE RIGHT TECHNIQUE," WHICH IS SCHEDULED FOR RELEASE IN NOVEMBER, 1996.

_____CHECK HERE AND RETURN IF YOU WOULD LIKE INFORMATION ON "SOCCER, THE RIGHT TECHNIQUE" VIDEO OR THE BOOK "GOALKEEPING UNDER TEN, THE RIGHT TECHNIQUE."

ORDER FORM

To order "Soccer, The Right Technique" send your check or money order for $14.95 plus $2.50 per book shipping and handling, or $1.25 per book shipping and handling for orders of 12 books or more, to:

"Soccer, The Right Technique"
1164 Bishop St., Suite 124 Box 1
Honolulu, Hawaii 96813

PLEASE PRINT:

Name_____

Address_____Apt. #_____

City_____State_____Zip_____

Telephone Number (   )_____

QTY	TITLE	UNIT PRICE	TOTAL
	Soccer, The Right Technique	$14.95	
	Postage & Handling ($2.50 per book, $1.25 per book for orders of 12 or more)		
	Hawaii residents add 4% sales tax		
	Please allow 4 to 6 weeks for delivery. TOTAL		

WATCH FOR T. J. MARTIN'S UPCOMING BOOK TITLED, "GOALKEEPING UNDER TEN, THE RIGHT TECHNIQUE," WHICH IS SCHEDULED FOR RELEASE IN NOVEMBER, 1996.

_____CHECK HERE AND RETURN IF YOU WOULD LIKE INFORMATION ON "SOCCER, THE RIGHT TECHNIQUE" VIDEO OR THE BOOK "GOALKEEPING UNDER TEN, THE RIGHT TECHNIQUE."

FE